To the little darlings Sameer, Sreya and Rishi who are growing up in the UK, with the hope that this book will help them to know their motherland – U.R.

For Shapan Adnan and family, Nasir Uddin Yousuff and Farid Majhi of Dhaka Theatre – P.D.

First published in Great Britain and the USA in 2009 by
Frances Lincoln Children's Books, 4 Torriano Mews,
Torriano Avenue, London NW5 2RZ
www.franceslincoln.com

British Library Cataloguing in Publication Data available on request

ISBN: 978-1-84507-918-5

Set in Hiroshige

Printed in China

1 3 5 7 9 8 6 4 2

B is for Bangladesh

Urmi Rahman

Prodeepta Das

F

FRANCES LINCOLN
CHILDREN'S BOOKS

Author's Note

I left Bangladesh, my motherland, more than two decades ago and since then I have made my second home in London. But every day I think about my beloved country. I miss the clear blue sky, the monsoon rains, the rivers, the green paddy-fields, the birds and the flame-red flowers that bloom in spring.

Bangladesh, a country of 56,000 square miles, was once part of India – part of the state of Bengal – but during the partition of India it became East Pakistan. Then in 1971, after a nine-month-long war, it emerged as the People's Republic of Bangladesh. So Bangladesh is a young country, but it has an ancient history and centuries of tradition.

It is a lush green land with many rivers, hilly areas in the north-east and the Bay of Bengal in the South. Most people live in villages and are Muslims, but many different religions exist side by side. The official language is Bangla (Bengali) and there are also many regional dialects. In spite of frequent flooding and other natural disasters, Bangladeshi people are amazingly resilient and welcome everyone with a smile.

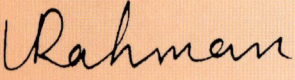

BANGLADESH

Dhaka

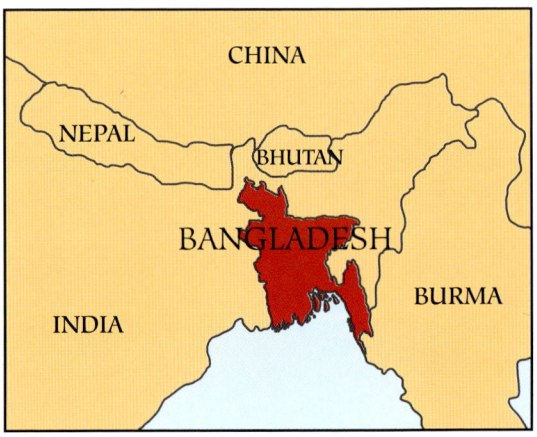

CHINA

NEPAL

BHUTAN

BANGLADESH

INDIA

BURMA

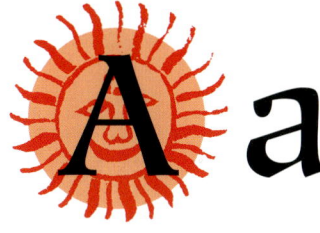 **A a** is for Ankhee – eyes. Mothers decorate their children's eyes with kohl, and put a black kohl spot on their baby's forehead to keep away any evil eyes.

 is for Bangladesh, a young, south Asian country lying between India and Burma. Rivers criss-cross the country, among them the mighty Padma and Jamuna rivers which flow into the Bay of Bengal. Bangladesh has the world's largest mangrove forest, the Sundarbans, where tigers roam. Most Bangladeshi people are Muslims, but there are also Hindus, Christians and Buddhists. We are all Bengalis and we speak a language called Bangla.

C **c** is for crocodile – which we call *kumir*. It can be seen basking on river banks and waiting for its prey, camouflaged by twigs and flotsam in the water. Crocodiles appear in many Bangladeshi children's stories.

 **D** **d** is for Dhaka, the country's capital city. Dhaka has some beautiful buildings, old and new. The most striking modern building is Parliament House. The park in front of the building is a popular place for family outings.

 **E e**

is for Ektara, a one-stringed
musical instrument played by
folk singers known as *bauls*.
Its body is made from a kind
of gourd. The baul holds the
ektara close to his ear and
strums it as he sings.

Ff

is for ferry, a large boat carrying people, cars, buses, lorries and even animals across and up and down the river. Bangladesh is a country of rivers, so it is a good way to travel.

Gg

is for Golap – the rose. Sweet-scented golap is used to weave garlands, to make the perfume attar and also rose-water – which is sprinkled on sweet dishes at festivals and on special occasions.

H h is for Horeen – a deer. Beautiful spotted deer known as Chitral Horeen can be seen grazing in the Chittagong hills and the Sundarbans, always on the alert and ready to sprint away at the smallest sign of danger.

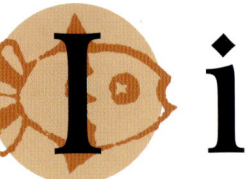 **I i** is for Ilish, our national fish. It has lots of small bones but is very tasty, especially when we cook it with mustard. At New Year, no celebration dinner is complete without ilish. The best ilish is found in the waters of the Padma river.

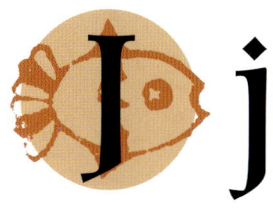

J j

is for Jamdani, a traditional Bangladeshi saree. It is woven by hand with geometric or floral designs. Nowadays, jamdani designs are used in scarves, kurtas (long shirts), turbans and tablecloths.

K k

is for Kana Machhi or "Blind Fly", a children's game. One child is blindfolded and the others circle round chanting the rhyme "O blind fly, catch whoever you can," while they touch the child and run away. The child stays blindfolded until he or she has managed to touch one of the others.

 **L l** is for Lungi, a man's cloth, worn rather like a wrap-around skirt, often with a check design. Villagers wear them all the time, but city men only wear them indoors.

 m

is for Market, the hub of village life. People from nearby villages gather to buy and sell groceries, vegetables, fish and meat. Special livestock markets are held for cattle, and during the Muslim festival of Eid-ul-Adha you often see people haggling over the price of animals to be slaughtered and cooked.

 n

is for Napit, the barber. You can find him in a small cabin or by the roadside, with an umbrella to cover his customer. Some village households still employ the same family of napits they have had for generations. A napit's shop is the place for catching up with the latest gossip.

 **O o**

is for Orna, a long piece of cloth worn by a girl to cover her head and shoulders. It is made from silk or cotton, decorated with all kinds of designs, and is extremely colourful.

P p is for Paddy, the rice plant. We grow it throughout the year. The rich silt carried down from the Himalayas in the rivers makes the soil rich and perfect for growing paddy. Paddy fields stretch as far as you can see. Everyone celebrates the harvest festival, Nabanna, with a feast of rice dishes.

Q q

is for Quilla, a fort. The Lalbagh Quilla in Dhaka is five hundred years old. Pari Bibi, the daughter of a Mughal governor, died at the fort and is buried there.

 **r** is for Rickshaw, the cheapest way to get around. Special artists decorate our rickshaws with pictures of animals, flowers, film stars and scenes of village life. Each rickshaw only has room for two people, but sometimes three or four climb on, and the rickshaw-man has to pedal much harder!

 **S s** is for Shapla or water lily – our national flower. People not only use them as decorations, they also cook parts of the plant as a vegetable and fry the seeds to make a delicious snack.

T t

is for Tabla, a pair of small drums which play an important part in any musical performance or dance. The tabla beats provide the rhythm, and the tabla player can adjust the strings on their tabla to make the beats sound high or low.

**U u** is for Utsav, a festival – and there are lots of them throughout the year in Bangladesh. The Hindu festival of Kumari Puja, held each year at the Ramakrishna Mission in Dhaka, is spectacular. Thousands of people gather to worship Kumari, a specially chosen young girl who sits up on a throne garlanded with flowers and wearing a crown.

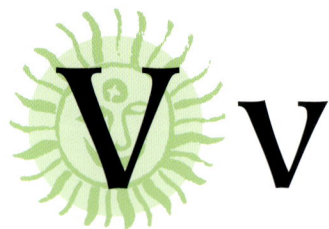**V v** is for Vihar, a Buddhist monastery and university. Somapura Vihar in the north-west is the largest vihar in south Asia and dates back to the 7th century. Excavations have unearthed a warren of rooms where Buddhist monks once meditated and slept.

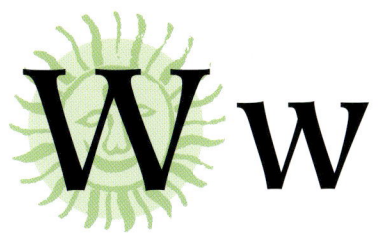 **W w**

is for Waterfall, and the one at Madhabakunda in Sylhet is the largest in Bangladesh. People go there to swim and splash about in a pool formed by the water gushing down from the steep cliff above. You can hear the noise of the waterfall a long way off!

 **x**

is for Cox's Bazar, a strip of land in the south which has the longest beach in Asia. Some visitors take a dip in the sea, others enjoy a leisurely stroll or just sit under their parasols listening to the rolling waves and watching crimson crabs scurrying to their holes in the sand.

 **y**

is for Yoke, or *langal*, which cuts furrows in the fields. It is made from wood and bamboo with a metal blade to cut into the soil. All over Bangladesh you can see farm workers urging on their bullocks using a langal.

Z·z is for Zhinuk, or sea shells. Children scour the beaches for zhinuk and treasure them. Some sell their finds to craftsmen who turn the shells into costume jewellery and beautiful decorations.